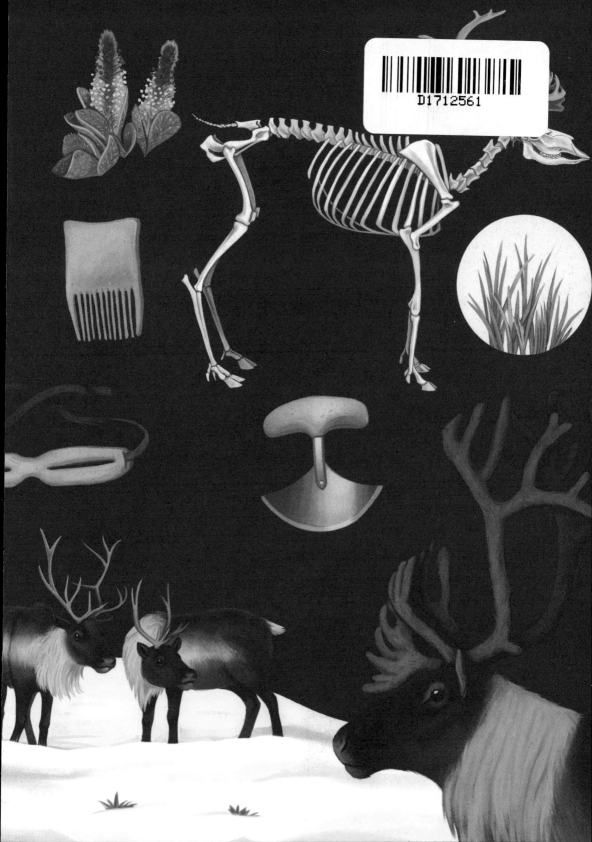

·ANIMALS ILLUSTRATED·

Caribou

·ANIMALS ILLUSTRATED·
Caribou

by Dorothy and David Aglukark • illustrated by Amanda Sandland

INHABIT
MEDIA

Note to Readers: For Inuktitut-language resources, including pronunciation assistance for Inuktitut terms found in this book, please visit inhabitmedia.com/inuitnipingit

Published by Inhabit Media Inc.
www.inhabitmedia.com

Inhabit Media Inc. (Iqaluit) P.O. Box 11125, Iqaluit, Nunavut, X0A 1H0
(Toronto) 191 Eglinton Avenue East, Suite 310, Toronto, Ontario, M4P 1K1

Design and layout copyright © 2019 Inhabit Media Inc.
Text copyright © 2019 by Dorothy and David Aglukark
Illustrations by Amanda Sandland copyright © 2019 Inhabit Media Inc.

Editors: Neil Christopher, Kelly Ward
Art Director: Danny Christopher
Designer: Astrid Arijanto

We acknowledge the support of the Canada Council for the Arts for our publishing program.

This project was made possible in part by the Government of Canada.

ISBN: 978-1-77227-234-5

Printed in Canada

Library and Archives Canada Cataloguing in Publication

Title: Caribou / by Dorothy and David Aglukark ; illustrated by Amanda Sandland.
Names: Aglukark, Dorothy, author. | Aglukark, David, author. | Sandland, Amanda, illustrator.
Series: Animals illustrated.
Description: Series statement: Animals illustrated
Identifiers: Canadiana 2019008068X | ISBN 9781772272345 (hardcover)
Subjects: LCSH: Caribou—Juvenile literature. | LCSH: Caribou—Behavior—Juvenile literature.
Classification: LCC QL737.U55 A35 2019 | DDC j599.65/8—dc23

Canada

Canada Council
for the Arts

Conseil des Arts
du Canada

Table of Contents

The Caribou

Caribou are members of the deer family. They are the only deer species in which both the males and females have antlers.

There are four types of caribou that live in Canada—barren ground caribou, Peary caribou, woodland caribou, and Grant's caribou. Barren ground caribou are the most common type of caribou in Canada.

Barren ground caribou have small ears and a short muzzle covered in hair. These features help the caribou retain heat in the cold Arctic climate. Barren ground caribou have the largest antlers of all Canadian caribou when compared to their body size.

A female barren ground caribou, called a "cow," will usually weigh about 200 pounds (about 90 kilograms), while a male, called a "bull," can weigh more than 300 pounds (about 140–150 kilograms).

Let's learn more about caribou!

Range

Barren ground caribou are found throughout Nunavut, in the Northwest Territories, and in northern parts of Manitoba and Saskatchewan at certain times of the year.

All types of caribou migrate, which means they travel very long distances at different times of the year to find food or give birth to their babies.

Barren ground caribou are known for travelling very long distances. They travel hundreds of miles in the spring to have their babies and find food. There are no trees in the Arctic, where the caribou live in the spring and summer, but in the fall and winter they travel south to the treeline, the northernmost area of land where forests can grow, to spend the colder months there.

Skeleton

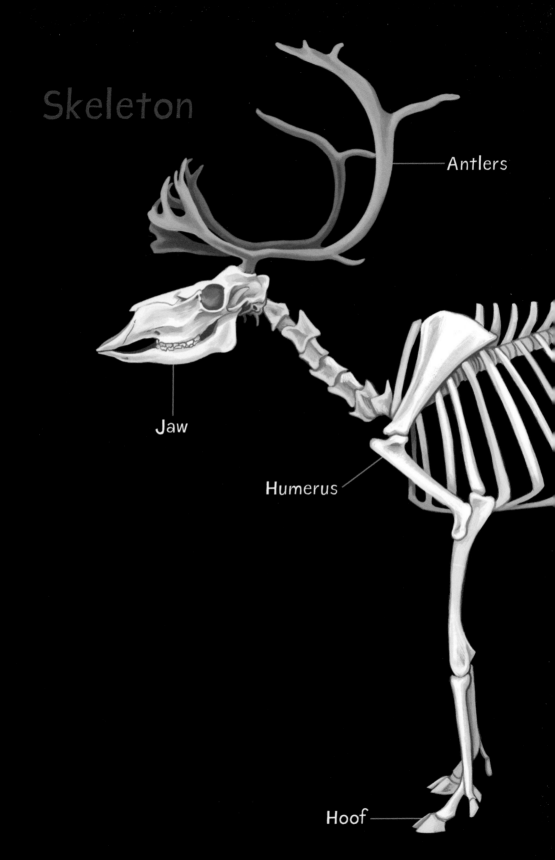

Antlers

Jaw

Humerus

Hoof

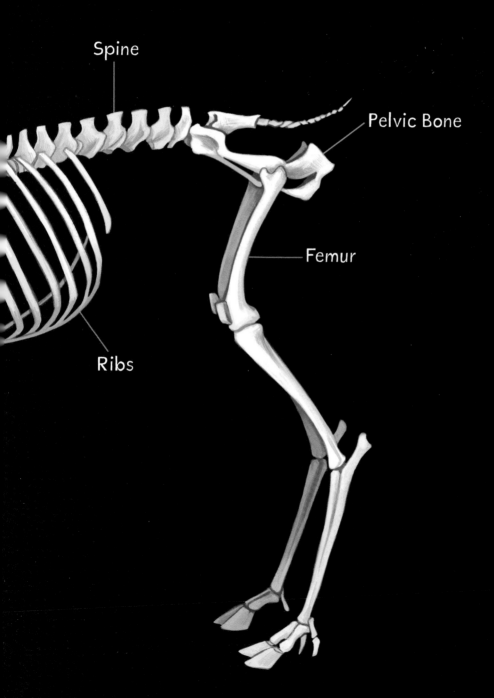

Spine

Pelvic Bone

Femur

Ribs

Teeth

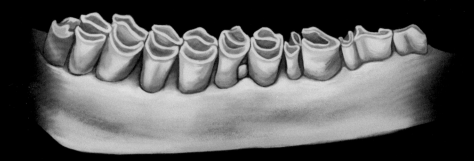

Caribou have large, flat teeth that are perfect for slowly grinding down plants. Like cows and goats, caribou belong to a group of animals called "ruminants." This means they chew their food for very long periods of time, bringing it up again and again to be broken down by their wide, flat teeth.

The teeth of ruminants are often ground down by their constant chewing. Because of this, their teeth are always growing!

Tooth

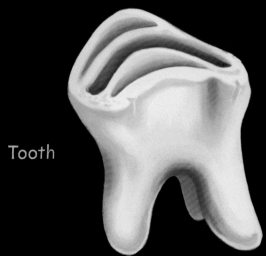

Male barren ground caribou have long antlers that reach outward as they grow, while females have smaller antlers that curve inward. Both male and female caribou use their antlers for defence against other animals, such as polar bears, wolves, and wolverines. Male caribou also use them to fight each other for the attention of females.

Caribou shed their antlers, meaning that the antlers fall off at a particular time of year. Male barren ground caribou lose their antlers in November or December. Females keep their antlers much longer and can carry their antlers throughout the winter months. In the spring, the antlers start to grow again and are fully grown by the end of summer.

Caribou antlers are covered in a soft, fuzzy material called "velvet."

Velvet

Diet

Caribou are herbivores, animals that only eat plants. The caribou's main food source is lichen, a plant that grows mostly on rocks.

Barren ground caribou arrive in Nunavut to have their babies just in time for the lichen to bloom, giving them easy access to food. When the herds migrate back to the treeline in the fall, the forest provides lots of lichen to eat. Caribou can use their hooves to help them dig lichen and other plants from beneath snow and ice.

Grass   Arctic Willow

Caribou can also eat other plants, such as grassy plants and willow leaves.

Babies

Baby caribou are called "calves." Caribou have their calves in special places called "calving grounds." Caribou herds travel very long distances every year to reach their calving grounds in the spring. Calving grounds are often protected places where people are not allowed to hunt caribou.

Caribou calves can walk a few hours after they are born. They drink milk from their mothers for the first few weeks before they are able to eat plants like the older caribou.

Caribou babies are very playful. They jump and run together while the rest of the herd is moving across the tundra. Caribou mothers are always very watchful over their playful babies to make sure they stay away from danger.

The Herd

Caribou live in herds of differing sizes depending on the season. During the winter months, male and female caribou live in separate groups, with the young caribou staying with their mothers. In the spring, the groups join together to make their long migration.

There are eight distinct herds of barren ground caribou in Canada. The largest of these herds is the Qamanirjuaq herd, with several hundred thousand members.

Arctic Wolf

Travelling in a large herd is safer than travelling in smaller groups because there are more animals to fend off predators, like wolves or wolverines. Each herd—no matter how large—also has a leader to guide the group safely on their migration.

Wolverine

Communication

Inuit have known for generations that caribou herds are led by one lead caribou. The rest of the herd is always watching the lead caribou for guidance. This caribou communicates to the others when it is safe to walk, and when they should stay still. The lead caribou could be a male or female.

Lead caribou are always on the lookout, trying to ensure the safety of the herd. A lead caribou has been seen testing the water of a lake with its hoof before it would allow the herd to cross. When the leader determined the water unsafe, the entire herd changed direction and did not cross the lake.

When a herd is in danger, caribou will release a scent from a gland in their hooves. The scent travels throughout the herd, letting the animals know that they are in danger.

Fun Facts

Caribou are very fast! They can run between 37 and 49 miles per hour (between 60 and 80 kilometres per hour). That helps them outrun animals that want to hunt them. Caribou have also been known to run for long distances trying to rid themselves of annoying mosquitos and other bugs in the summer months.

Hoof

Caribou are strong swimmers. Adults can swim between 4 and 6 miles per hour (between 6.5 and 10 kilometres per hour) when they need to. They have large hooves that act as paddles to help move them quickly through the water.

Inuit Uses for Caribou

Caribou are a very important animal in traditional Northern life. They were traditionally hunted with bows and arrows and continue to be hunted by modern means today. Caribou meat is one of the most important country foods in the Inuit diet.

Traditionally, Inuit would use a familiar tool to help hunt caribou: the *inuksuk*! By placing lots of *inuksuit* lined up in the hills at various levels, hunters could control where a caribou herd walked and get the herd to move in the direction they wanted the herd to go. The caribou would become confused, perhaps thinking an inuksuk was a person, and not walk toward it!

Comb   Snow Goggles   Ulu

In addition to eating the meat, Inuit have many uses for parts of the caribou. Caribou skin is still used to make various items of clothing and was used traditionally as bedding in an *iglu* or *qarmaq*, and as diapers for babies. Caribou bones and antlers were used to make tools such as combs, snow goggles, and parts of an ulu.

Dorothy and David Aglukark are elders from Arviat, Nunavut.

Amanda Sandland is an illustrator living in the Toronto area. She studied illustration at Seneca College, eventually specializing in comic arts and character design. When not drawing, she can be found studying, designing characters, creating costumes and replica props, or burying her nose in a comic.

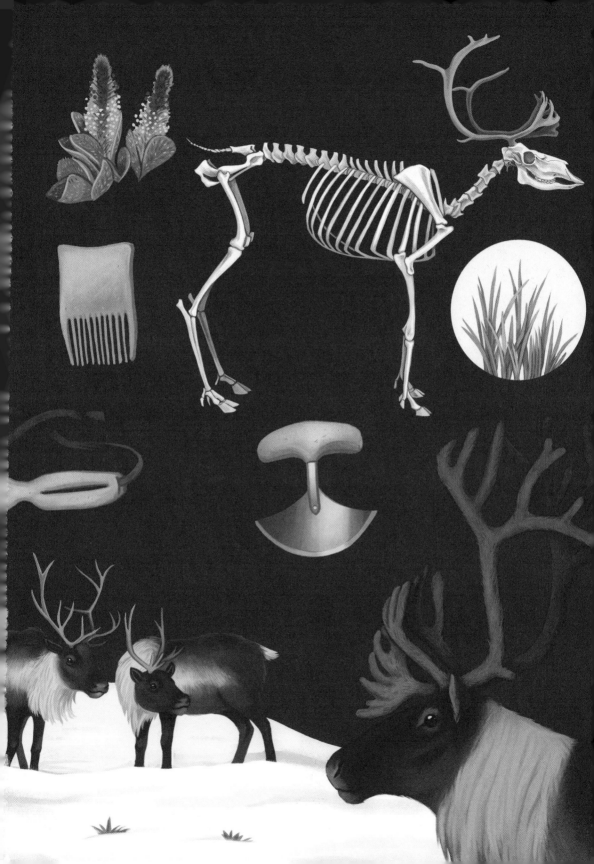